FUN AND GAMES

MAZES

Perimeter and Area

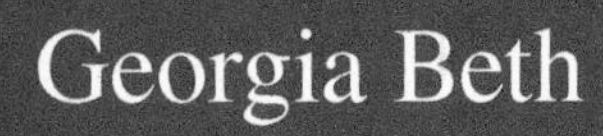

Georgia Beth

Consultants

Michele Ogden, Ed.D
Principal
Irvine Unified School District

Colleen Pollitt, M.A.Ed.
Math Support Teacher
Howard County Public Schools

Publishing Credits

Rachelle Cracchiolo, M.S.Ed., *Publisher*
Conni Medina, M.A.Ed., *Managing Editor*
Dona Herweck Rice, *Series Developer*
Emily R. Smith, M.A.Ed., *Series Developer*
Diana Kenney, M.A.Ed., NBCT, *Content Director*
Stacy Monsman, M.A., *Editor*
Kevin Panter, *Graphic Designer*

References Cited: Roberson, Gary T. 2004. "Creating a Crop Maze with GPS." North Carolina Cooperative Extension Service.

Image Credits: p.7 (inset) Courtesy of Arthur Bagumyan, Magic Jump Rentals Inc.; p.9 Sion Touhig/Getty Images; p.10 Skyscan Photolibrary/Alamy Stock Photo; p.11 Piotr Nowak/AFP/Getty Images; pp.12–13 Medioimages/Photodisc/ Getty Images; p.13 Europics/Newscom; p.14 (bottom) dpa picture alliance/ Alamy Stock Photo; pp.14–15, 15 (front) Photos by Lucien Marcs; p.16 Photo courtesy of Cherry Crest Adventure Farm, Ronks (Lancaster County) PA. www. CherryCrestFarm.com; p.17 (top and inset) Maze installation by artist group Trouble (Sam Hillmer and Laura Paris), Photo by Walter Wlodarczyk, (bottom) Photo by Kevin Allen; p.18 Floresco Productions/Getty Images; p.19 (upper right) Courtesy of Seth Cooley, Cool Patch Pumpkins; pp.20 (inset), 20–21 Rex Features via AP Images; p.23 Photo courtesy of Spoon & Tamago; p.24 Jay Boucher; p.26 Andy Adamatzky; all other images from iStock and/or Shutterstock.

Library of Congress Cataloging-in-Publication Data

Names: Beth, Georgia, author.
Title: Fun and games : mazes / Georgia Beth.
Description: Huntington Beach, California : Teacher Created Materials, [2018] | Includes index. | Audience: Grades: 4 to 6.
Identifiers: LCCN 2017012263 (print) | LCCN 2017040571 (ebook) | ISBN 9781480759435 (eBook) | ISBN 9781425855611 (paperback)
Subjects: LCSH: Maze puzzles--Juvenile literature. | Labyrinths--Juvenile literature.
Classification: LCC GV1507.M3 (ebook) | LCC GV1507.M3 B48 2018 (print) | DDC 793.73/8--dc23
LC record available at https://lccn.loc.gov/2017012263

Teacher Created Materials
5301 Oceanus Drive
Huntington Beach, CA 92649-1030
http://www.tcmpub.com

ISBN 978-1-4258-5561-1

Table of Contents

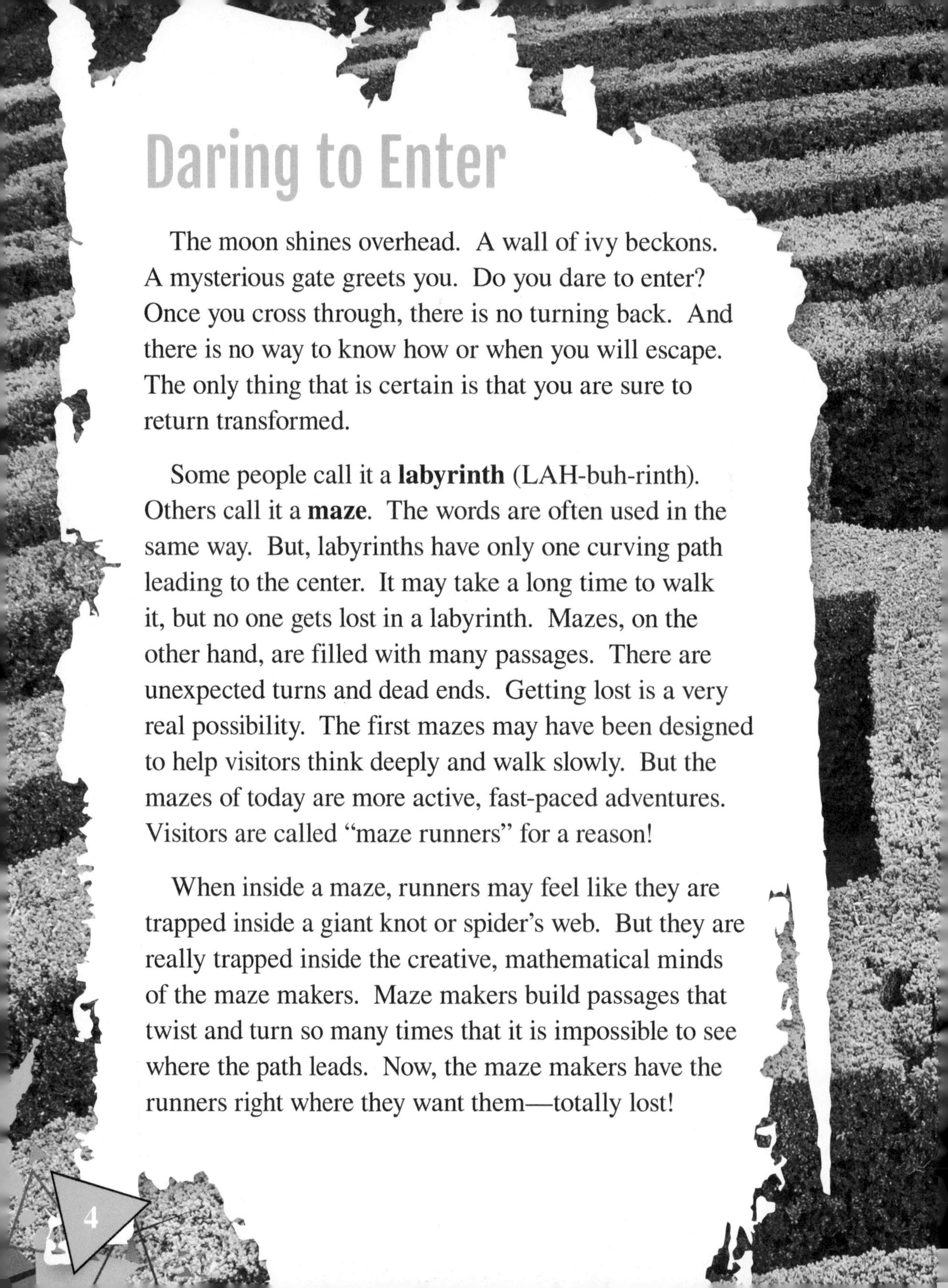

Daring to Enter

The moon shines overhead. A wall of ivy beckons. A mysterious gate greets you. Do you dare to enter? Once you cross through, there is no turning back. And there is no way to know how or when you will escape. The only thing that is certain is that you are sure to return transformed.

Some people call it a **labyrinth** (LAH-buh-rinth). Others call it a **maze**. The words are often used in the same way. But, labyrinths have only one curving path leading to the center. It may take a long time to walk it, but no one gets lost in a labyrinth. Mazes, on the other hand, are filled with many passages. There are unexpected turns and dead ends. Getting lost is a very real possibility. The first mazes may have been designed to help visitors think deeply and walk slowly. But the mazes of today are more active, fast-paced adventures. Visitors are called "maze runners" for a reason!

When inside a maze, runners may feel like they are trapped inside a giant knot or spider's web. But they are really trapped inside the creative, mathematical minds of the maze makers. Maze makers build passages that twist and turn so many times that it is impossible to see where the path leads. Now, the maze makers have the runners right where they want them—totally lost!

A boy searches for the exit in a hedge maze.

overhead view of a hedge maze

Plan It and Pay for It!

Being inside a maze can be intimidating. The walls hide the exit, and escape is uncertain. But, fly high above to get a **bird's-eye view**, and mazes look much simpler. The way out is clear. This is how **designers** visualize mazes before they are built.

Every maze starts as a sketch on paper. Builders work out where to place the edges of mazes. Each line is a wall or dead end that forces people to make a decision. Left or right? Forward or backward?

Designers use their imaginations to create places that interest visitors. After planning the size and shape of a maze, materials are chosen. There are living mazes made of corn, hay, or other plants. Wood, cardboard, and stone have all been used to build mazes. There are also mazes of mirrors, which make escape really hard!

maze building materials

Designers use materials in creative ways. They form some mazes in interesting shapes. They make others look like they are made out of desserts, such as cake and ice cream. The materials are not real, so the pieces do not melt. But the effect is still totally sweet!

LET'S EXPLORE MATH

Many people rent inflatable mazes for parties. The maze shown is a rectangle with a length of 30 feet. Its **area** is 1,080 square feet.

1. What is the width of the maze?
2. What is the **perimeter** of the maze?

Along with size and materials, maze makers look at location. It is important to choose a **site** that is easy for people to find. And it helps when the land is flat enough for walking.

It can take anywhere from a few hours to a few years to build a maze. So, builders want to be sure the work will be worth it. A **budget** shows how much the process will cost. Expensive materials and workers' wages can add up. But, a great maze can bring in thousands of people each year. That can mean a lot of money for the owners!

After the design and budget are finalized, it is time to build the maze. Workers post flags or lay down patterns to mark a maze's location. This is the outline. It's like a map showing workers where to create passages. The crew works together to build the walls. Gary Roberson, a professor from North Carolina State University, says the process is like "connecting the dots."

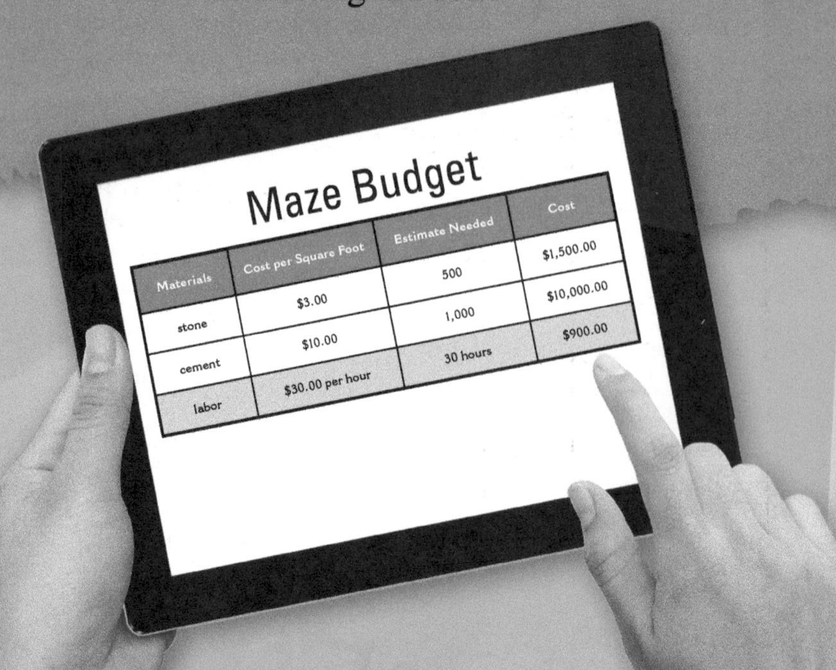

Maze Budget

Materials	Cost per Square Foot	Estimate Needed	Cost
stone	$3.00	500	$1,500.00
cement	$10.00	1,000	$10,000.00
labor	$30.00 per hour	30 hours	$900.00

Some companies sell patterns for corn mazes to farmers. Imagine that a farmer wants to plant a corn maze in a field. The field is a rectangle with a length of 90 meters and a width of 60 meters. The farmer hopes to use a maze pattern with an area of 6,000 square meters. Will the maze pattern fit in the field? Why or why not?

60 m

90 m

Workers build a maze out of straw bales.

bird's-eye view of a corn maze

Bigger and Better?

When maze makers decide to build a maze, they do not just want to build any maze. They want to build a better, bolder maze! They set out to create the best maze ever built. But before they begin building, it helps to measure the length and width of the maze's planned location. This lets the designers know how much space they have for the design. The bigger the space, the better it is for designers to create their masterpieces.

But for runners trying to solve a maze, bigger may not always be better. When they are lost, walking the length of a maze can feel like an eternity. Maze designers often visit the sites where they build mazes so they can walk around to get a feel for the size. That way, they know how perimeter will affect the design. They also know how it will affect the maze runners.

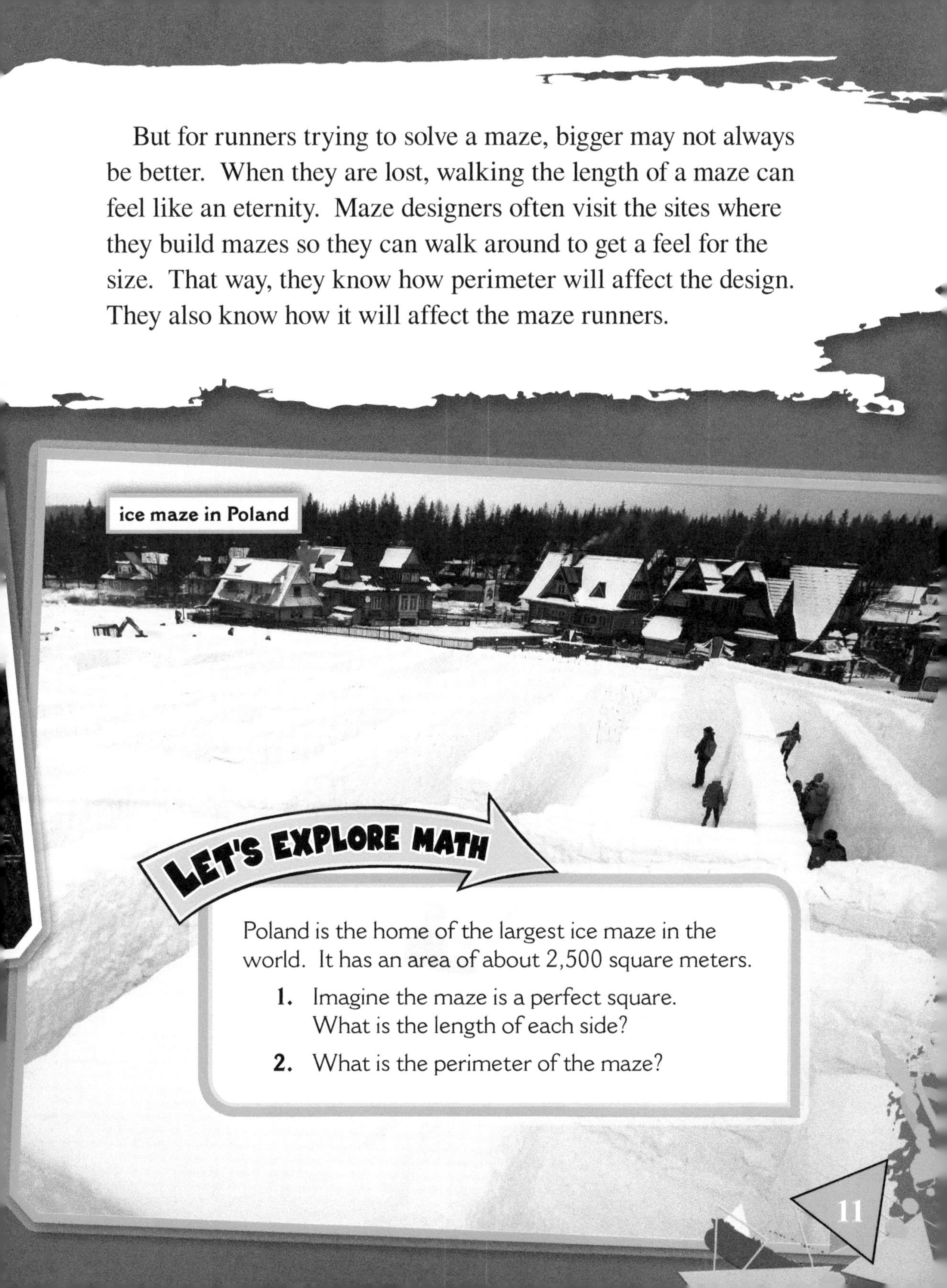

ice maze in Poland

LET'S EXPLORE MATH

Poland is the home of the largest ice maze in the world. It has an area of about 2,500 square meters.

1. Imagine the maze is a perfect square. What is the length of each side?
2. What is the perimeter of the maze?

Still, the biggest mazes draw people from around the world. It feels good for runners to say that they have conquered these puzzles!

The Dole Plantation in Hawaii has the world's largest permanent hedge maze, made from 14,000 Hawaiian plants. The Pineapple Garden Maze covers more than 137,000 sq. ft. (12,700 sq. m). And the path is almost $2\frac{1}{2}$ miles (4 kilometers) long!

The Pineapple Garden Maze has fresh flowers along the path, and a sculpture of a golden pineapple lies at the center. It takes most people less than an hour to solve the maze. The fastest maze runners win a juicy prize. And, their names are recorded for all to see.

Pineapple Garden Maze

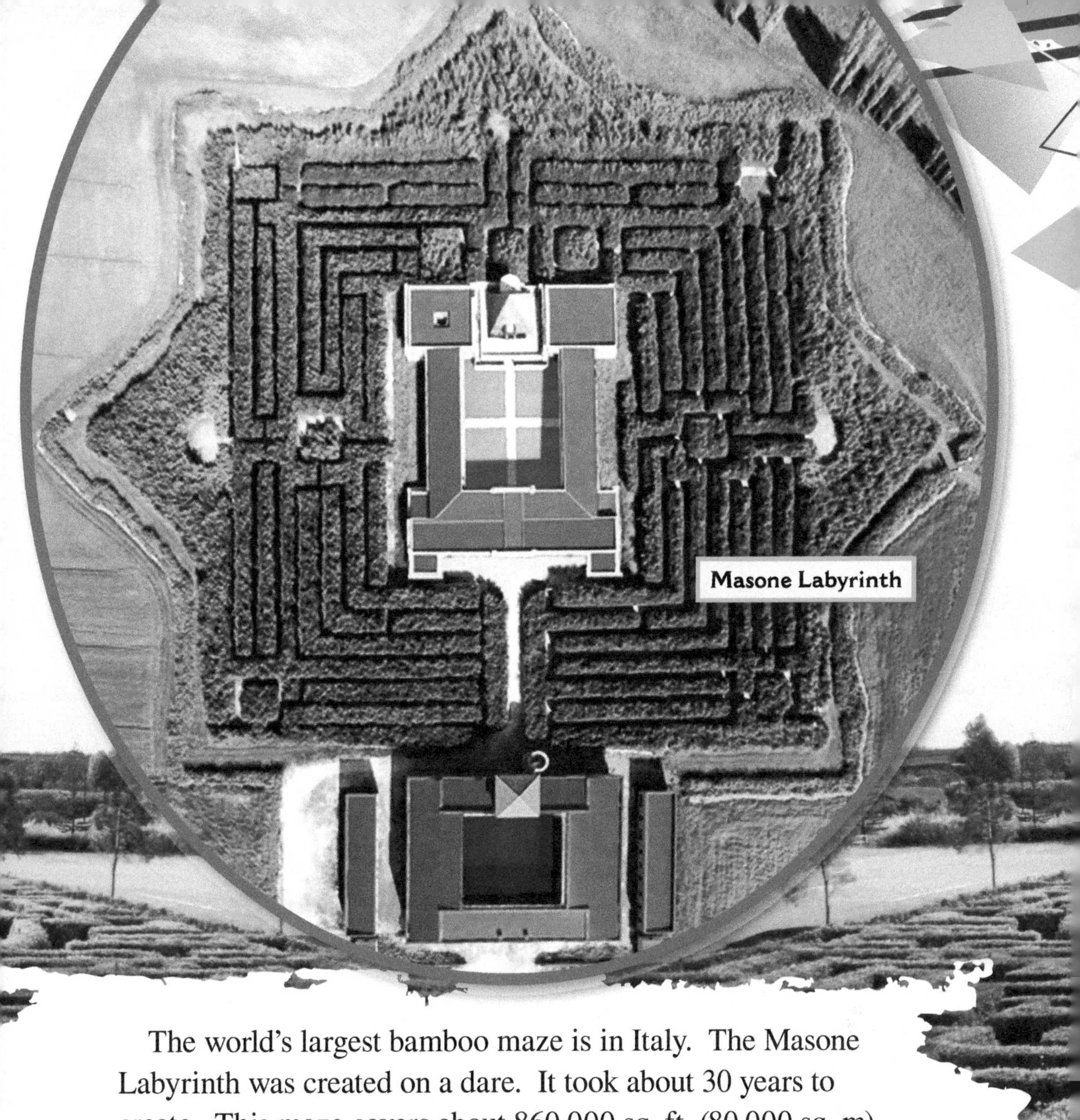

The world's largest bamboo maze is in Italy. The Masone Labyrinth was created on a dare. It took about 30 years to create. This maze covers about 860,000 sq. ft. (80,000 sq. m). That is about the same size as 15 football fields! A perfect square sits in the middle of a star. Hundreds of thousands of bamboo plants form the walls. The builder wanted to create a place that would fill people with wonder—done!

Filling in the Blanks

Remember that bird's-eye view? People can see the outline or perimeter of a maze by looking down at it. It is important for maze makers to know the distance around the maze. But that is not where the action is. The adventure takes place in the space between the outer walls of the maze.

Maze makers are mathematicians who see the world in square units. Seeing the world this way makes it possible for maze makers to imagine mazes everywhere they look. They might see small, simple mazes on sheets of paper. They might see large mazes in fields of corn.

corn maze in France

Ian Anderson and his six-story maze

Maze maker Ian Anderson sees mazes in places other people don't. He even saw a maze on the walls of a stairwell. He drew a maze in the stairwell of the Cartoon Network building. Although Anderson came across some dead ends and went in circles at times, it only took him a few hours to solve his six-story maze!

A space's area determines the possible area of a maze. Area is the amount of space covered by square units inside shapes. It is the space surrounded by perimeter. But area isn't just something that is found in squares on a sheet of graph paper. It is what designers use to bring mazes to life.

In Queens, New York, maze makers created a see-through maze made of twine. The maze was harder to solve than it looked! So, musicians and dancers were invited to perform in the center of the maze. The performances encouraged maze runners to keep going.

If a twine maze seems too easy, the Cherry Crest Corn Maze in Ronks, Pennsylvania, is sure to test even the best maze runners. First, runners are given a game board and instructions. Then, they begin winding their way to the middle. Along the way, runners have to find clues, play games, and solve puzzles to move forward. It takes most people about an hour to complete the $2\frac{1}{2}$ mi. (4 km) pathway. Two staff members wander through the maze all day to keep people from getting lost. Think you can memorize the route for next year? Think again. The designers change the maze's shape and clues every year to keep people guessing.

Cherry Crest Corn Maze

This twine maze in Queens, New York was created by artists Sam Hillmer and Laura Paris.

LET'S EXPLORE MATH

Some mazes aren't outside. The twine maze was built inside of a 50,000 square foot room. The BIG Maze was another indoor maze. This square maze measured 60 feet on each side. If there was nothing else inside of it, would the BIG Maze have fit in the room that the twine maze was in? Why or why not?

the BIG Maze in Washington, DC

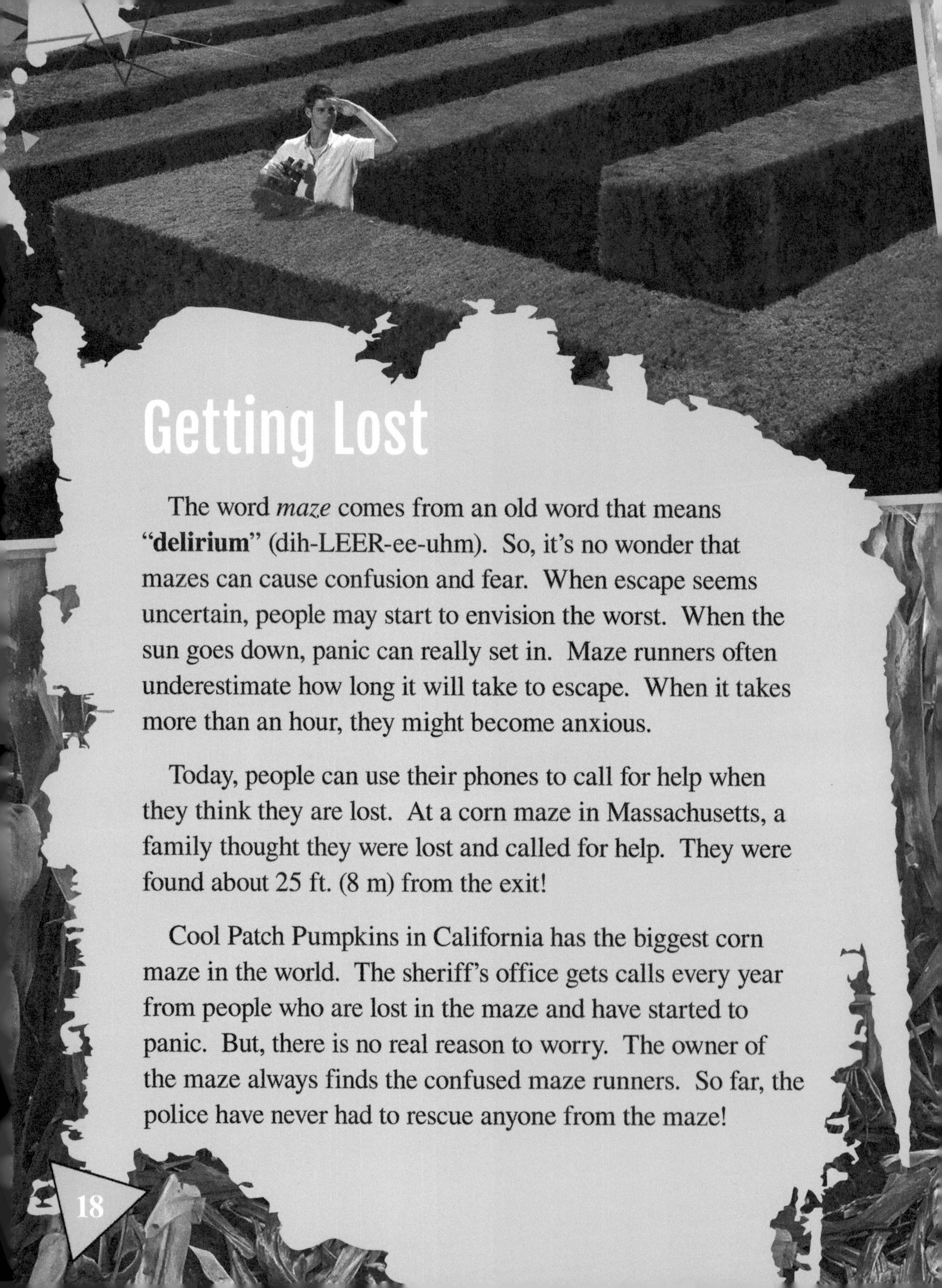

Getting Lost

The word *maze* comes from an old word that means "**delirium**" (dih-LEER-ee-uhm). So, it's no wonder that mazes can cause confusion and fear. When escape seems uncertain, people may start to envision the worst. When the sun goes down, panic can really set in. Maze runners often underestimate how long it will take to escape. When it takes more than an hour, they might become anxious.

Today, people can use their phones to call for help when they think they are lost. At a corn maze in Massachusetts, a family thought they were lost and called for help. They were found about 25 ft. (8 m) from the exit!

Cool Patch Pumpkins in California has the biggest corn maze in the world. The sheriff's office gets calls every year from people who are lost in the maze and have started to panic. But, there is no real reason to worry. The owner of the maze always finds the confused maze runners. So far, the police have never had to rescue anyone from the maze!

A father leads his daughters through a corn maze.

Some maze runners like the feeling of getting lost. The Mirror Maze in London used more than its walls to disorient visitors. Curving halls, tunnels, dead ends, and staircases to nowhere added to the drama. Maze runners solved the tricky maze while seeing their reflections everywhere and finding the oval doors that led to other rooms.

The best mazes are difficult to solve. But they are not impossible. A maze with a lot of dead ends is actually one of the easiest to solve because there are fewer paths to test. If runners have to retrace their steps more often, solving the maze becomes more difficult. There is a greater chance of getting lost.

Many maze runners try to avoid getting lost by only taking right turns. Another tactic is to keep one hand on the maze's wall at all times. The trick to this method is to remember to put a hand on the wall as soon as you enter. And whatever you do, don't let go! If you take a wrong turn and then try this approach, you'll just keep going in circles!

Designer Es Devlin stands near an oval door in the Mirror Maze.

Es Devlin and her Mirror Maze

LET'S EXPLORE MATH

Imagine that the Mirror Maze is in the shape of a rectangle with an area of about 1,000 square meters. Find the dimensions of a rectangle with this area. Then, find the perimeter of your rectangle.

PAC-MAN® was developed in Japan in 1980.

Other Maze Experiences

Some mazes are large enough to walk through. But, walking is not the only way to experience a maze. Some video games rely on mazes to take players on digital **quests**.

Of course, not all mazes use technology. But, don't count them out just yet. These mazes can still be very difficult. *Maze: Solve the World's Most Challenging Puzzle* is a 96-page picture book published in the 1980s. It is filled with riddles, puzzles, and a giant maze. There was a $10,000 prize for the first person to solve the riddle hidden within the maze. But after two years, no one had solved it! Finally, the money was split between the people who were closest to the end.

Another maze from the 1980s was released on social media in 2013. The **intricate** maze was 30 years old and drawn by hand. Photographs show layers and layers of tiny pathways. So far, no one has solved this maze. All that is known for sure is that a janitor in Japan created it. He secretly drew for seven years.

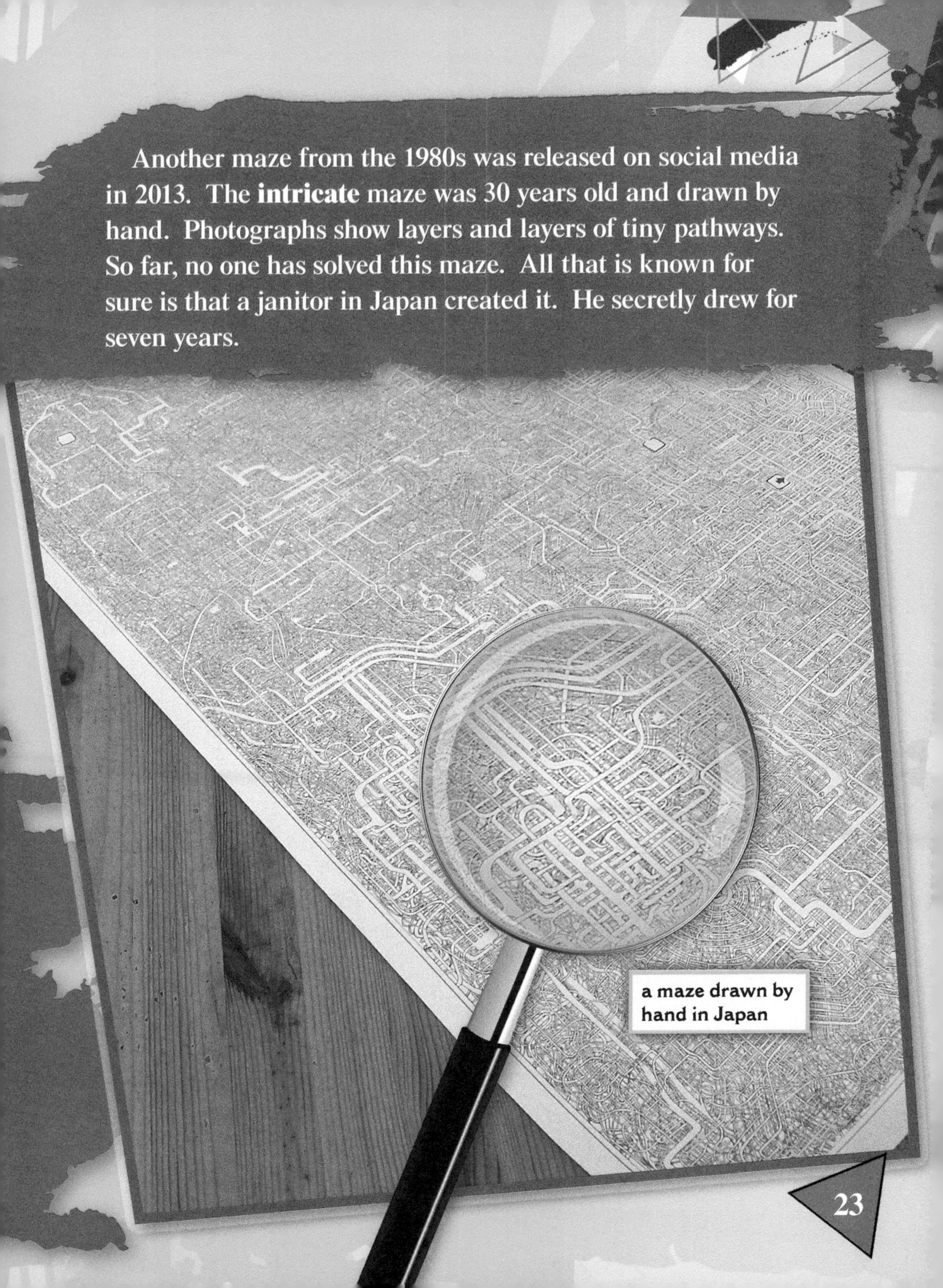

a maze drawn by hand in Japan

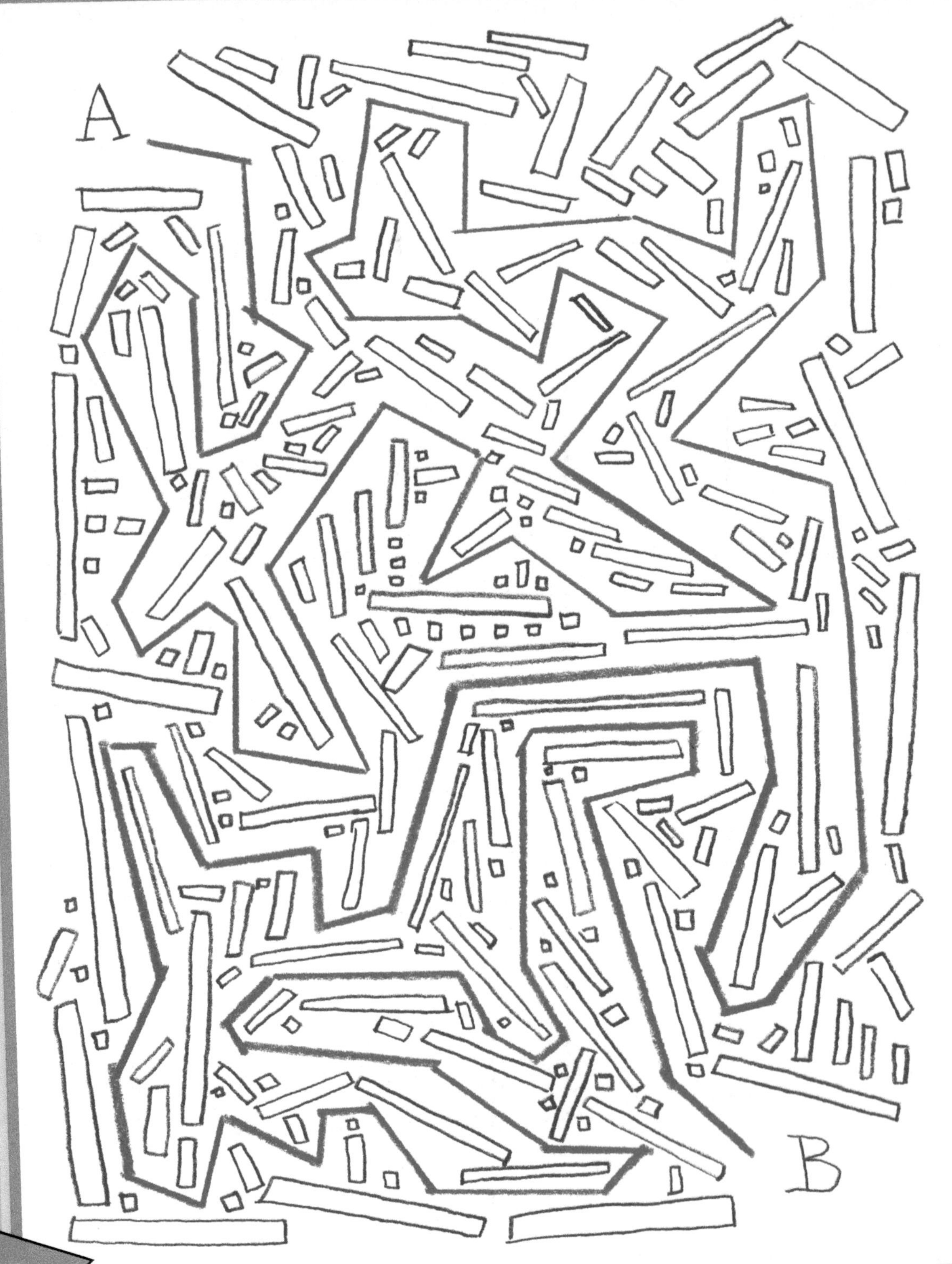
A
B

Want to have total control over the maze experience? Try your hand at making your own maze. There are websites that help people generate mazes quickly. But it might be more fun to draw one by hand. Maze makers can lose themselves in the process, just like solvers do.

Following a few guidelines can help you make a maze that intrigues people. First, grab a ruler and graph paper. Do your best to make the width of the passages the same throughout. Start by drawing straight passages. Then, try drawing curved routes. Next, practice drawing **junctions**. At these points where passages meet, you force the maze solver to make a decision. So, avoid drawing junctions that lead to obvious dead ends. Keep it surprising. Balance the turns that lead to dead ends and the passages that backtrack to earlier parts of the maze. Linking groups of winding passages, called **vortexes**, can also make a maze more difficult.

As you draw, be sure to check that the maze works. It is very easy to mistakenly create a maze with no solution. If the maze still feels too easy, you can always change exit routes to dead ends.

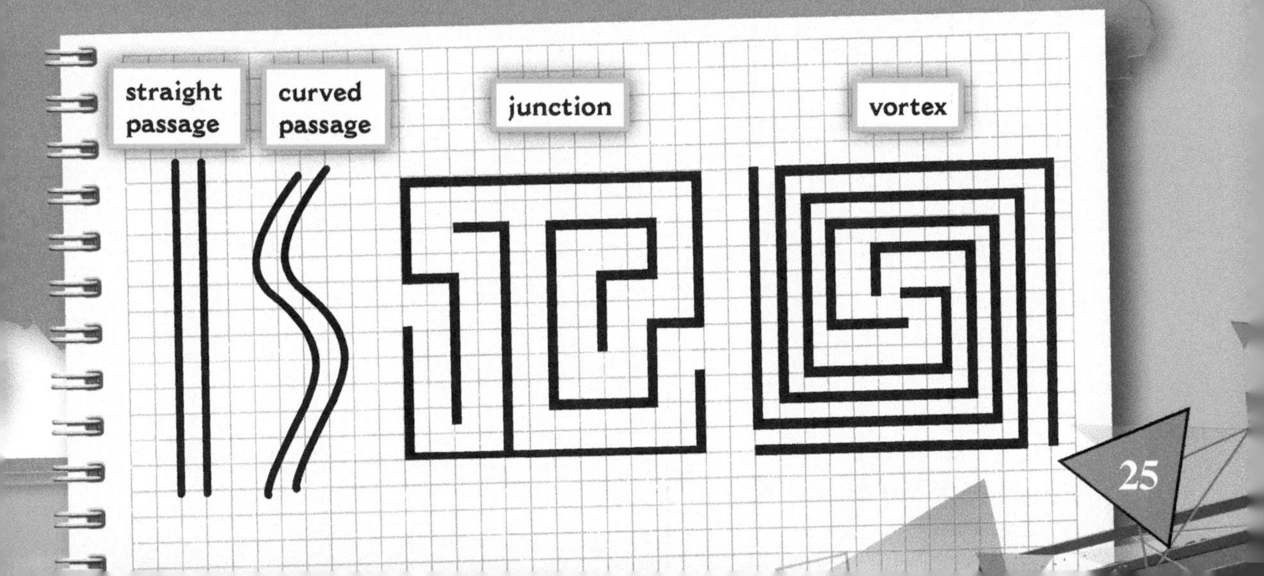

Looking for a Way Out

Creating a maze requires a balance of logic, math, and art. Solving a maze is about staying calm and being **strategic**. But, humans are not the only ones with those skills! Scientists use mazes to learn how animals think. Lab rats search for food and show how well they remember a path when tested again. Lizards wind their way through mazes looking for sunlight. Even simple, brainless slime molds can escape a maze. Their trail of goo marks where they have been. Then, they avoid sliding across those paths later. Just like human maze runners, these animals are always looking for a new way out.

The magic of making a maze and trying to solve one is the feeling that comes from not knowing the solution. It is the mystery that draws people in. Is this the way out? Or, is that? A feeling of accomplishment makes designers and solvers crave more.

Whether you draw a maze, look at one from above, or find your way deep inside a vortex, you may find that mazes are a-*maze*-ing!

A slime mold solves a maze.

A lab rat finds its way through a maze in search of food.

Problem Solving

Now, it is your turn to design a maze! Use 1-centimeter graph paper to draw a rectangular maze. Be sure to follow the guidelines on page 25.

1. What will you call your maze? Where will your maze be located? What material will you use to build it?
2. What is the area of your maze design? What is the perimeter?
3. Draw a rectangle that has half of the area of your maze design. What is the perimeter of the rectangle? Show your thinking.
4. Draw a rectangle that has double the area of your maze design. What is the perimeter of the rectangle? Show your thinking.

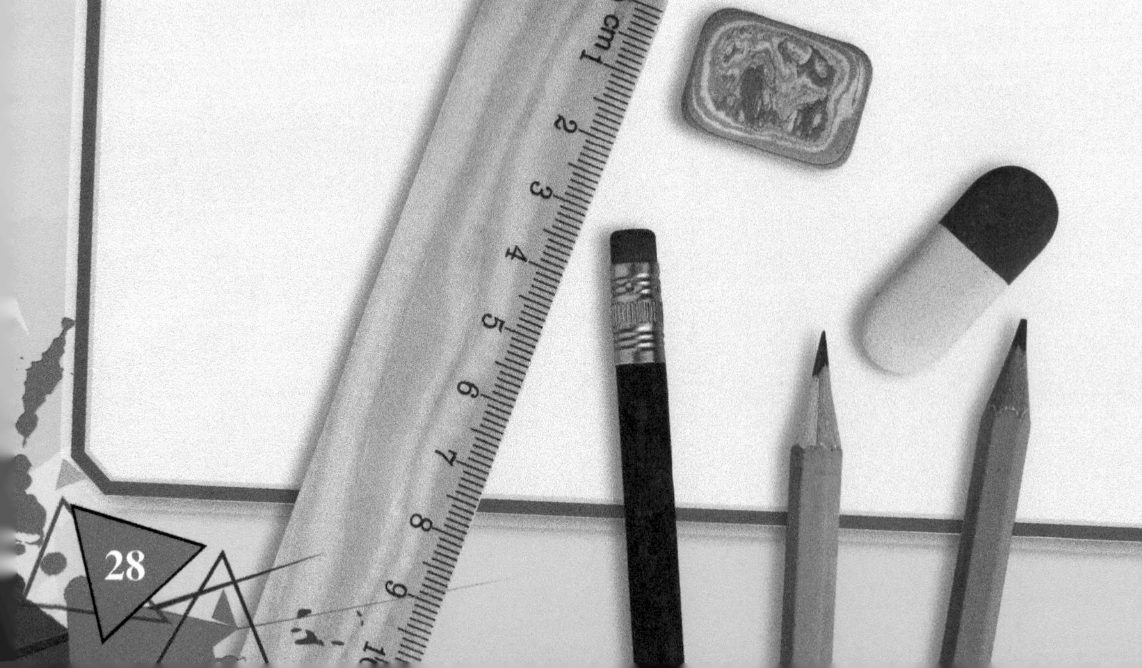

Glossary

area—the amount of space covered by square units inside a two-dimensional shape

bird's-eye view—a view from above

budget—a plan for using money over a period of time

delirium—a mental state of wild excitement, happiness, and often confusion

designers—people who plan how something will look and be made

intricate—having many complex parts

junctions—places where two things come together

labyrinth—a place with a curved pathway that winds toward the center before the exit

maze—a complicated and confusing system of pathways that twist, turn, and form dead ends in surprising ways

perimeter—the distance around the outside of a shape

quests—journeys made in search of something

site—the location of something

strategic—relating to a careful method for achieving a particular goal

vortexes—pathways that wind around a central location

Index

Answer Key

Let's Explore Math

page 7:

1. 36 ft.
2. 132 ft.

page 9:

No; The field has an area of 5,400 sq. m, so the area of the pattern is greater than the area of the field.

page 11:

1. 50 m
2. 200 m

page 17:

Yes; The BIG Maze had an area of 3,600 sq. ft., so it had an area less than 50,000 sq. ft.

page 21:

Answers will vary, but the length and width of the rectangle must have an area of 1,000 sq. m and a perimeter accurate for the dimensions given. Example: a 40 m by 25 m rectangle has a perimeter of 130 m.

Problem Solving

1. Answers will vary, but should include a title of the maze design, a location, and materials.
2. Answers will vary, but should show the area as the number of sq. cm and the perimeter as the sum of side lengths in cm.
3. Answers will vary, but the area of the rectangle should be half of the number of sq. cm of the original maze design and the perimeter should be the sum of side lengths in cm.
4. Answers will vary, but the area of the rectangle should be double the number of sq. cm of the original maze design and the perimeter should be the sum of side lengths in cm.